Wendy the Water Drop

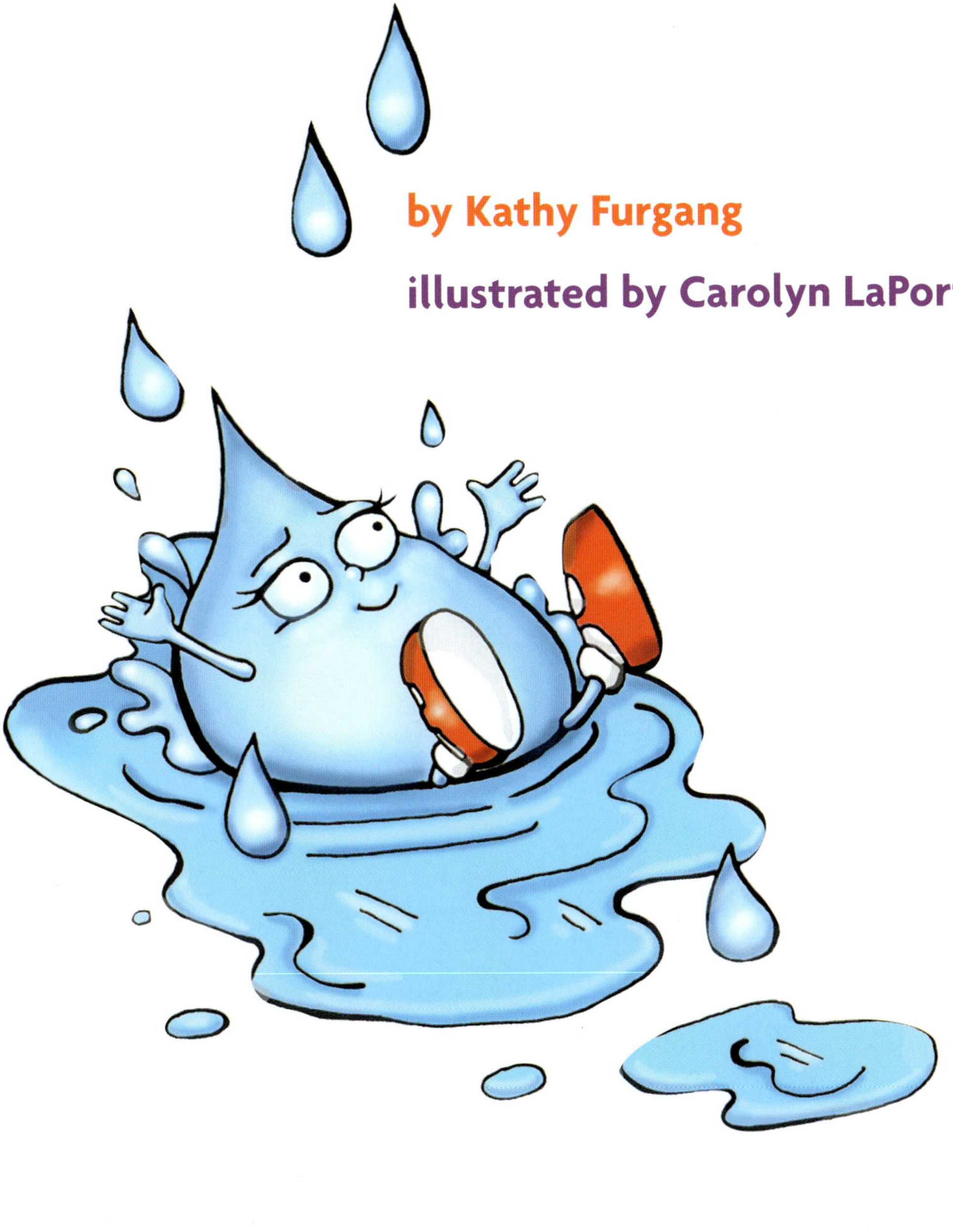

by Kathy Furgang

illustrated by Carolyn LaPorte

This is Wendy.
She is a drop of water.

Right now Wendy is in a cloud, but she won't be there for long. She is always on the move.

Wendy and her friends fall from the cloud as rain.

They hit the ground. Now Wendy is part of a puddle.

The sun comes out. Where has Wendy gone?

Wendy is back up in the air.
She is in a new cloud.

Oh, oh.
It is getting cold.
It looks like snow is coming!

Wendy has turned into a beautiful snowflake! There is no other snowflake like her.

Now Wendy is part of the snow on the ground. A boy makes Wendy into a snowball.

He throws the snowball at his friend. Pow!

The sun comes out. After a few days, the snow melts. Wendy is water again.

Where will Wendy go next?

Soon Wendy is going very fast.

Now Wendy is part of a river.
The river goes on and on.

The river flows into the ocean.
Wendy likes the ocean.
She hopes she can stay here a long time.